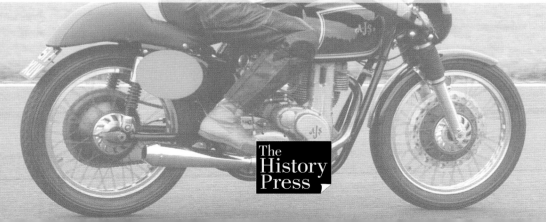

The British Motorcycle Story

Colin Jackson

The History Press

Published in the United Kingdom in 2013 by
The History Press
The Mill · Brimscombe Port · Stroud · Gloucestershire · GL5 2QG

British Library Cataloguing in Publication Data
A catalogue record for this book is available from the British
Library.

Hardback ISBN 978-0-7524-8735-9

Typesetting and origination by The History Press
Printed in India
Manufacturing managed by Jellyfish Solutions Ltd

CONTENTS

ACKNOWLEDGEMENTS

I would like to thank Tony East (proprietor of the excellent A.R.E. Motorcycle Museum in Kirk Michael), Job Grimshaw, Bill Bewley, Richard Blackburn, Carsten Hoefer, Guenter Kranz, Adrian Pingstone, Brian Wigmore, Ronald Jennings, Robin Vincent-Day, Paul D'Orleans (aka The Vintagent), and all those others who kindly told me the stories of their machines, gave me cups of coffee and generally treated me in the friendly and helpful way typical of British bikers.

Grace's Online Guide to British Industrial History is a superb and free repository of knowledge on all things British and mechanical – highly recommended.

Any errors spotted by the army of knowledgeable enthusiasts out there are entirely my own.

Today, we are familiar with the motorcycle in many forms; it ranges from the low-powered pizza delivery moped, to scooters, small commuter bikes, powerful sports machines and tourers, all the way to MotoGP racers.

Most of these bikes have something in common; they are not made in Britain. A few, mainly top-end models, such as Ducati and Aprilia, come from Italy, but the majority are Japanese, with the 'big four' companies – Honda, Suzuki, Yamaha and Kawasaki – dominating the market.

However, it has not always been this way. For much of the twentieth century, British motorbikes ruled supreme and (mostly) British designers and engineers made that possible. This is the story of the 'golden age'. Along the way there may well be a few surprises.

If something moves, somebody will want to race it. If that something is as exciting as a motorcycle then competition will always be a vital part of its story.

It was therefore natural that, from the very beginning, manufacturers would seek to sell their products by proving them in competition with other makes. Speed was not always the only factor, though, as the buying public also wanted reliability and ease of handling. Events to test these elements rapidly became important, alongside out-and-out races; trials demonstrated the machines' agility and toughness, while

endurance runs for prizes such as the Maudes Trophy showed that standard machines could run without problems over long distances. This latter is awarded by the Auto Cycle Union (ACU) for outstanding performances by standard machines, and is given directly to manufacturers. It was first awarded in 1923 (to Norton) and most recently in 1994 when a team of ten New Zealanders averaged over 100mph on Yamaha machines during the Junior Isle of Man TT. In between, the trophy has been won by many of the British makers featured in this story.

◄ ► 348cc AJS 7R. This is one of the great British racers, introduced in 1948. The 7R was effectively reintroduced in 1958 as the 500cc Matchless G50, both marques having been absorbed into the AMC group.

➤ Matchless G50. The later 500cc version of the AJS 7R.

Did you know?

The last victory for a single-cylinder machine in a 500cc Grand Prix was that of Godfrey Nash in the 1969 Yugoslavian GP – on a Cammy-powered Norton Manx. The factory had retired from Grand Prix racing in 1954, but the Manx Norton continued to win races in private hands, and still does so in classic events all over the world.

When it started to handle really well, they knew it was broken
Simon Smith, owner of a pre-featherbed Manx Norton

Trials riding has produced its own 'greats'; Marjorie Cottle was considered one of Britain's best riders in the 1920s, while the exploits of Sammy Miller on his 500cc Ariel HT5 made even its number plate (GOV 132) famous. In later years, the Lampkin dynasty continued this tradition.

As early as the 1920s, trials events in Britain diversified into a new form of racing over rough ground, which came to be known as 'scrambling'. This is now an international sport in its own right and is known as 'motocross'; the name deriving from the French word 'motocyclette', and the words 'cross country'.

Of course, pure racing on tarmac has always been a major draw due to its combination of speed and danger. Whether on the great banked circuits such as Brooklands in England or Montlhéry in France, or on the many shorter tracks which exist in most parts of the world,

every kind of machine from the Bantam to the Superbike is raced. The FIM World Championship (MotoGP) is seen by many as the pinnacle, and riders such as Lorenzo, Pedrosa and Stoner are household names even as Handley, Duke, Ivy and Hailwood were in their day.

Through it all runs the Isle of Man TT (along with its amateur partner, the Manx Grand Prix). Such is the place of the Isle of Man in motorcycle history that any motorcyclist referring simply to 'the island' will expect to be understood.

The TT is the oldest motorcycle race in existence and has been described by no less a person than Murray Walker (whose father himself won fifteen silver replicas in the event) as the greatest motorsport event of any kind in the world. It no longer has World Championship status due to the dangers inherent in racing modern bikes on closed public roads, but racers still

Did you know?
Any rider who managed to lap the Brooklands circuit at over 100mph was awarded a Gold Star lapel badge. Wal Handley achieved this in 1937 on a BSA Empire Star, and this was the origin of the 'Gold Star' range of BSA sports machines. The 'Star' designation had been used for many yeas to indicate a tuned 'sports' engine; such engines carried a red star mark on the timing cover.

queue for entries. There were over sixty competitors in the Newcomers race at the 2012 MGP. With an eye to the future, there is now a race for electric machines at the TT, and the 100mph lap has been achieved in this event.

The story of the motorcycle does not have a clear 'beginning'. The bicycle could be considered as the real starting point, but of course this could be traced back to the invention of the wheel! Instead, I will start with the effective re-invention of the wheel by an English scientist/engineer.

Sir George Cayley, 6th Baronet of Brompton (1773–1857), was the first to identify the four forces of flight: lift, drag, thrust and weight. He built a successful manned glider and is sometimes referred to as the father of aerodynamics. He was also the inventor of the tension-spoked wheel. He realised in 1808 that a wheel in which the forces were absorbed through tension rather then compression could be made lighter, and that this would be an advantage when building an aircraft undercarriage. Cayley strung his wheels with 'tight cording'.

These wheels were improved in 1849 by the use of wire for the spokes by another Englishman, George Stanley.

James Starley and William Hillman also used them on their Ariel bicycles from 1870. They were used on virtually all motorcycles until the arrival of cast alloy wheels in the 1970s, and they are used today on bikes such as the current Triumph Thruxton.

Inevitably, it was the internal combustion engine which actually transformed the carriage into the car, and the bicycle into the motorbike, and both therefore began at roughly the same time. Both also began in roughly the same place – Germany. In fact, the first production motorcycle is generally accepted to have been the Hildebrand and Wolfmuller (H&W) of 1894.

The H&W used the rear wheel as a flywheel and its two cylinders were directly connected to this, so that in effect the rear

the pedals. Various engine positions were tried, such as the centre of the rear wheel, above the front wheel and under the seat, but fairly quickly the engine settled in the bottom bracket, just where the cyclist's pedals had long been. Many of the key players in our story established themselves at this early stage.

In 1886, a pair of German immigrants, Siegfried Bettmann and Mauritz Schulte, renamed their London-based company the Triumph Cycle Company, and in 1888 they established a factory in Coventry. The first Triumph motorcycle rolled out in 1902 and one of the best-known British motorbike manufacturers was thus born of German parents.

Velocette motorcycles are among the most highly regarded of classic british machinery. Veloce were a company owned and run by the Goodman family, and were based for much of their existence in Hall Green,

of the bike was all part of the engine. In spite of this, however, the overall appearance is of a powered bicycle.

In the early days, engineers, some trained and others working in garden shed workshops, tended to start from the bicycle frame and general layout, while adding an engine to either supplement or replace

Birmingham, though the family name was originally Gutgemann. The company was always small compared to the likes of BSA and Triumph, and production was therefore fairly limited, yet, at any modern meeting of classic bike enthusiasts, the Velocette is always well represented.

The Birmingham Small Arms Company (BSA) diversified into motorcycle manufacture (again via bicycles) in 1910 and, as a major engineering firm, was well placed to take its place as a major player. Oddly enough, the chairman of the company in the latter part of the 19th century was one John Goodman, although he was born in Peterborough.

The Stevens Screw Company built their first prototype motorcycle around the turn of the twentieth century using an American engine, and later produced their own engines which they supplied to other motorcycle makers. Later, in 1909, Joe Stevens formed the AJS company (A.J. Stevens & Co. Ltd) in Wolverhampton to build a bike for the TT.

James Norton formed his company in Birmingham in 1898 and produced his first motorcycle in 1902, manufacturing his own engines from 1908.

However, it wasn't all about businesses which were to become household names. A relatively small number of large companies also supplied engines and gearboxes to those whose names appeared on the fuel tank, and there were plenty of these

Only a biker knows why a dog sticks his
head out of a car window.
Anon

smaller manufacturers to supply. An article in *Motorcycle News* (MCN) (7 May 2009) states, for example, that J.A. Prestwich (JAP) supplied engines for 137 different machines. This author admits he hasn't checked that figure, but it is likely that two-stroke specialists Villiers may even have exceeded it!

Many of these 'cycle' companies were eventually bought out and became part of more long-lived firms, while others simply went out of business. Nevertheless, many of these companies contributed ideas and engineering breakthroughs far in excess of their modern-day fame.

There is clearly not room in a book of this size to even list all of these, so what follows is a personal 'pick of the best' and an attempt to demonstrate how the modern motorcycle came to be.

The Calthorpe company began in Birmingham as a bicycle maker in the last years of the nineteenth century, diversifying into cars from 1904 and motorcycles after 1909.

The bike in the picture overleaf is a 'Junior' model, dating from the time of the First World War. It has a single-cylinder, air-cooled, four-stroke 'Precision' engine made by F.E. Baker Ltd of Kings Norton, Birmingham. This company supplied engines to a number of bicycle manufacturers in Britain and elsewhere. The machine had a two-speed gearbox and a leather belt to drive the rear wheel. Note that the brakes were simple rubber blocks operated

Did you know?

In the early days, it was common for manufacturers to build only the cycle parts of their machines, fitting engines and gearboxes from other makers. Even the mighty Brough Superior was fitted with engines by JAP and Matchless, and gearboxes from Sturmey-Archer and Norton.

by cables – exactly as on bicycles – although the rear brake acts on the inner surface of the drive pulley.

Calthorpe produced their own engines from 1924 and the company survived until the start of the Second World War, at which time they were producing both solo and sidecar machines of advanced design. The range included 250cc, 350cc and 500cc machines of stylish appearance, capable of up to 85mph and with fuel economy approaching 100mpg.

Calthorpe's roots in bicycle manufacture were typical; the motorcycle began as a pushbike with an engine fitted to help the rider along. As these engines became more powerful, the rest of the bike had to improve to cope with the increased speeds.

If a simple solid-framed bicycle hits a bump at speed, the entire machine is likely to leave the ground. This was clearly dangerous and it was not long before attempts were made to improve the design. The Calthorpe Junior had an early front suspension system, as can clearly be seen in the photographs.

The Triumph Model H was a big success for the young company, being adopted by the military for service in the First World War. Triumph were already producing their own 4hp 550cc engine and their machine also had 'proper' front suspension. Telescopic forks and shock absorbers were still in the future, but a D-shaped 'girder' pivoted at the head bearing to act on a spring between the handlebars featured. This apparently crude arrangement resulted in a considerable change in the geometry of the bike as the suspension moved – even the wheelbase varied – but developments of the girder

◄ 1914 Calthorpe Junior.

➤ Right side view of 'Precision' engine in Calthorpe Junior showing the rudimentary carburettor and the flywheel cover.

➤➤ Left side view of 'Precision' engine in Calthorpe Junior showing the exposed inlet and exhaust valves and the drive pulley. Note the intricate construction of the leather drive belt. The lack of tension is due to the belt being removed from the rear pulley when the bike is not in use.

Triumph Model H
*c.*1914. 30 000 of these
machines were used by
British despatch riders in
the First World War
(photo: A. R. Pingstone).

system remained in use for many decades. Indeed, Phil Vincent (of whom much more later) continued to reject telescopic forks – themselves not free of vices – into the 1950s.

The model H also used a Sturmey-Archer, chain-driven, three-speed gearbox with a hand-operated lever. These gearboxes were to be popular in many motorcycles of the period; even used by the Brough Superior. The bike in the picture has a leather belt around the headstock, which was a military modification to improve the machine's durability by protecting the spring in hard use.

An alternative suspension was the 'springer' in which the fork itself is solid, but the wheel is then carried on a separate pivoted arm, or 'leading link', at the lower end. George Brough used this type of fork on his legendary SS100 and the layout can be clearly seen in the photographs.

Springer forks are sometimes seen today on American choppers.

A spring alone is not enough, however, as the bike will bounce for some distance after passing over a bump in the road unless some form of damping is added. The Manchester-made DOT (whose name means 'Devoid Of Trouble') shows an early solution to this. The fork movement is damped by a pair of friction plates clamped together. Later designs improved on this slightly by providing easier adjustment. The Brough Superior SS100, built in Nottingham, was considered to be the 'Rolls Royce of motorcycles' and the picture overleaf shows how the friction damper was fitted with a simple hand adjuster.

If you think this bike looks a bit special, then Colonel T.E. Lawrence (Lawrence of Arabia) certainly agreed. In a letter sent to George Brough in 1927, and later used

'The Rolls-Royce of motorcycles'. This Brough Superior, nick-named 'Moby Dick', sold shortly afterwards for £210,500 and became one of the ten most expensive motorcycles in the world.

in the company's advertising, Lawrence wrote:

> I'm not a speed merchant, but ride fairly far in the day (occasionally 700 miles, often 500) ... The riding position and the slow powerful turn-over of the engine at speeds of 50 odd, give one a very restful feeling.

How many of us would ride that far in a day today, on smooth roads and modern machines?

The bike illustrated, nicknamed 'Moby Dick', is interesting in a number of ways (apart from the obvious beauty of the plated frame!). It is fitted with a JAP

◀ Cantilever rear suspension on Brough SS100.

▶ Brough Superior springer fork with adjustable friction damper.

1142cc V-twin engine and a Norton four-speed, foot-change gearbox. The engine is original, though modified early on in its life, but the bike would have been fitted with a Sturmey-Archer three-speed gearbox when new. This was hand operated and many owners made the upgrade to the Norton box. In its original three-speed form, the bike was tested by *Motor Cycling* magazine

Did you know?

T. E. Lawrence owned no less than seven Brough Superiors. Sadly, it was his death while riding one which prompted the neurosurgeon Hugh Cairns to begin research which led to the widespread use of crash helmets.

in 1931 and achieved a top speed of 106mph (all SS100 models were certified by the factory as being capable of at least 100mph). With more tuning work carried out, it later reached 115mph – and 109mph in second gear!

When sold at auction by Bonhams in October 2011, the bike fetched £210,500 and became one of the top ten most expensive motorcycles in the world, though its exact position in the list depends on the currency used in the calculation and the current exchange rate.

The DOT deserves mention for more than its front forks, though. The Bradshaw oil-cooled engine used oil from the sump to cool the cylinder and main bearings. It gained the unflattering (and almost certainly unfair) nickname of 'oil boiler', but was used in a number of machines, including the DOT shown on page 32.

◀ The adjustable friction damper on 'Moby Dick'. The friction plates are compressed by the star-shaped spring washer. Turn the screw clockwise to increase the pressure, and hence the damping effect. This system was widely used on machines of the period though it is obviously not possible to adjust compression and rebound damping separately.

Colonel T. E. Lawrence, The Wonder-Man of the Great War

Previous to parting with his 5th " Brough Superior " in 1927 and going to ? ? ? who knows where !—Colonel J Lawrence wrote :

"Dear Mr. Brough,

Yesterday I completed 100,000 miles since 1922 on five successive "Brough Superiors," and I am going abroad very soon, so that I think I must make an end, and I thank you for the road pleasure I have got out of them . . . I have not had an involuntary stop, and so have not been able to test your spares service . . . Your present machines are as reliable and fast as Express Trains, and the greatest fun in the world to drive—and I say this after twenty years' experience of cycles and cars. . . . The "SS 100" holds the road extraordinarily. . . .

I'm not a speed-merchant, but ride fairly far in the day (occasionally 700 miles, often 500) and at a fair average, for the machine's speed in the open lets one crawl through the towns, and still average 40-42 miles in the hour. The riding position and the slow powerful turn-over of the engine at speeds of 50 odd, gives one a very restful feeling.

There, it is no good telling you all you knew before I did. They are the jolliest things on wheels.

Yours very sincerely,
(Signed) T. E. LAWRENCE."

Hundreds of delightful letters eulogising on the "Brough Superior" Machine and the "Brough Superior" Service may be seen at Haydn Road on request.

◻ ◻ ◻

" . . The Brough Superior After-Delivery Service is like the Bike, the best in the world. . . . ."
C. J. K.,
London.

now owns his **6th** " Brough Superior," having purchased every 1000 c.c. Model " Brough Superior " since 1922.

◄◄ This Brough advert from 1927 uses a strong recommendation from Lawrence of Arabia and states that he has just bought his sixth SS100 machine and has now completed 100,000 miles on them.

◄ The rider's view from an SS100.

▲►▼ The DOT B1 used a Bradshaw oil-cooled 344cc engine. Only the cylinder head requires cooling fins. The girder fork is fitted with a friction damper which requires a pair of spanners to adjust it. This would be necessary over time as the friction material wore away.

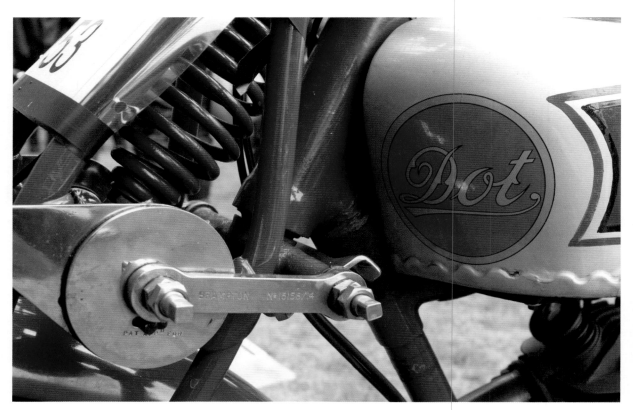

Note the smooth cylinder walls. Only the head carries cooling fins.

Granville Bradshaw was, in fact, an imaginative and experimental engineer, and it is perhaps for this reason that his failures are sometimes remembered more than his achievements. His toroidal engine occupied a great deal of his time but never made it to

People are more violently opposed to fur than leather because it's safer to harass rich women than motorcycle gangs.

Alexei Sayle

production, while the ABC Dragonfly radial design was once described as the engine which would have lost Britain the First World War had it continued another year. However, it is likely that this remark was actually a criticism of the Air Board's decision to put an untried engine into large-scale production, rather than a swipe at its design.

He was responsible in the 1920s for the ABC 400cc motorcycle, with its revolutionary horizontally opposed twin-cylinder engine. Such engines have been used extensively since, most notably in BMW machines.

Returning to the theme of front suspension, one major problem already noted is the tendency of the front end to 'dive' under heavy braking. This alters the geometry of the machine and therefore affects the steering, and is felt most seriously when a sidecar is fitted.

The English engineer Ernest Earles patented a design which eliminated dive and also enabled the wheelbase to remain virtually constant as the suspension moved. The Earles fork is a form of leading link, but the main fork is bent back so far that the moving link can be pivoted behind the wheel.

How does this prevent dive? As the brakes are applied, there is inevitably a tendency for the drum (or disc) to rotate forwards with the wheel and this has to be prevented by a torque arm attached to the fork. On the Earles fork, this torque arm

Happy Douglas rider after winning a time trial in August 1923 (courtesy of Grace's Guide).

can be attached in such a position that it lifts the fork.

Careful calculation of the various angles actually enables dive to be reduced, eliminated or even reversed, so that the front end rises under braking! As mentioned, the chief advantage of this system is on sidecar outfits and the Douglas Dragonfly illustrates it perfectly.

Russian-made Ural outfits use a leading link front suspension, but this is technically not an Earles fork as the pivot is not behind the wheel – the basis of the Earles patent. BMW used an Earles fork on solo bikes for many years, but these were designed to allow some dive as most solo riders prefer the greater 'feel' this gives under braking.

Of course, each maker has their own badge or logo. This is found on Douglas machines. The bikes were built in Bristol, but the family clearly remained proud of their Scottish roots!

This 1955 Douglas Dragonfly sidecar outfit shows the 'anti-dive' Earles Fork front suspension. The crucial torque arm attaching the brake drum to the main fork is easily seen.

The telescopic fork had actually made its first tentative appearance in the very early days of motorcycling. Alfred Scott, a brilliant and innovative engineer from Bradford, designed a twin-cylinder, two-stroke motorcycle which was built for him by the Jowett company, better remembered now for its cars such as the 'Jupiter' model. However, the modern telescopic fork with internal hydraulic damping was actually developed by BMW and did not appear on a British motorcycle until the B31 of 1945. The Scott, introduced in 1908, was well ahead of its time and not only had semi-telescopic forks, but was also equipped with a kick-starter at a time when riders of other makes had to be able to bump start them; no easy job as anyone who has done it will know. The Scott was also not fitted with pedals, as its designer was presumably confident they would not be needed. Possibly the most significant feature of all was the use of a water-cooled cylinder head; Scott having taken out the relevant patents. It took a little longer (though only until 1914) for the cylinders to also be contained within a full water jacket.

By 1910, Scott motorcycles even had a two-speed drive operated by a foot pedal. Scott and his machine were successful in hill-climb events; so much so that moves were made to have it banned. It was claimed that the two-stroke engine had an unfair advantage since it fired twice as often as the more conventional four-strokes. The machine was not banned, but a handicap was applied. The Scott bikes were deemed to have 1.32 times their actual capacity for competition purposes. Scott, a businessman as well as an engineer, made great use of this in his future advertising – the machine everyone else is afraid of!

Demand for Scott motorcycles now required him to set up his own factory in

◄ The Douglas outfit had a massively strong frame, swinging arm rear suspension and a surprisingly small 348cc flat twin to push it all along. Even in solo trim these bikes were not particularly lively performers. The sidecar looks comfortable though; it even has a glove compartment and a clock.

Suitable riding kit for a lady in 1911 (courtesy of Grace's Guide).

Front end of the Scott TT machine. Note the combination of trapezoid and telescopic elements even though the hydraulically damped telescopic fork was almost twenty years away.

The Scott 'flying squirrel' mudguard emblem.

WW 4459

▲ This machine was works bike number two for the cancelled 1928 sidecar TT and raced as a solo in 1930. It was also used for testing and later had a long racing career in private hands.

➤ 1947 Scott Squirrel. Spare spark plugs are carried under the seat. It is sad to note how similar to the 1928 machine this one is, though. Even a truly innovative company could become complacent.

44

A closer view of the later Scott.

Saltaire, a Yorkshire village on the River Aire founded by the enlightened Victorian mill owner Sir Titus Salt.

Scott's machines were highly successful in the Isle of Man, scoring TT wins in 1912 and 1913, and setting record lap speeds in several other years. The Scott in the photograph on page 44 is one of eight which were built by the factory for the Isle of Man TT in 1928. This was the number two machine for the sidecar event, but, as the race was cancelled, it was not raced that year. It was then registered for road use and used for practice and testing.

However, the new engine developed for the 1930 TT was not a success (I have heard it described more colourfully as a disaster) and the 1928 bikes, including this one, were eventually raced.

One of the riders, Bill Kitchen (later to become a prominent speedway rider), is recorded as having a minor 'off' at Creg-ny-Baa, a right hand corner at the end of the Mountain section of the course, and the Scott entries did not figure among the leading finishers.

The bike was then recorded as 'scrapped' by the factory, but in fact it was raced for more than twenty years by Cliff Kingham.

Restored to Concours condition in 2011, it is now back on the road.

Any consideration of British motorcycles (and particularly British motorcycle engines) must rapidly turn to the Triumph Speed Twin. Designed by Edward Turner, who was at the time both the chief designer and managing director of the Coventry company, the concept of a 500cc, four-stroke, overhead valve twin was not new. The frame into which this engine was originally bolted had a rigid rear end and a girder fork. And yet, this was the machine which transformed Triumph's fortunes and gave a whole new image to 'British bikes'

➤ Edward Turner's Triumph Speed Twin engine, which permanently redefined British motorcycles.

➤➤ The Triumph Tiger T100 SC. These 500cc machines are slightly lighter than the 650cc Bonneville and have a shorter wheelbase and steeper fork rake. The footrests are high and the seat relatively low. All these factors contributed to a good off-road performance.

The Triumph Trident was a three cylinder machine; effectively a 'Speed Twin and a half', intended to replace the ageing 650cc range of twins and to offer greater smoothness. The pictures show an impressive replica (by 'Wobbly Bob') of the most famous Triumph Trident of them all. Known as Slippery Sam, the original won five consecutive Production TTs before being destroyed in a museum fire.

– an image which remains strong to the present day. Why was this? Although not revolutionary in concept, the Twin had more power and torque than most of its single-cylinder competitors, and also weighed less. It also looked good; having the 'character' of the popular singles. The Japanese multi-cylinder bikes were still far in the future, but the realisation had dawned that for a given engine size, multiple lightweight pistons moving more quickly mean more power.

Did you know?
Marlon Brando rode a 1950 Thunderbird in the film *The Wild One*. While this may have given motorcyclists a threatening, anti-social image, it also gave a massive boost to the Triumph brand and set the scene for later 'biker' films.

In effect, this is similar to the two-stroke advantage; it gets the fuel in, burned and out again more quickly, and it also leads to a smoother-running engine.

The bike was introduced in 1937, but its real impact was made after the Second World War. Triumph's factory was destroyed on 14 November 1940 in the Coventry Blitz, along with a great deal of tooling and paperwork, and a new plant was built in Meriden.

By the end of the war, Triumph had supplied some 50,000 machines to the military, but it is the revamped Speed Twin which is most often credited with enabling the company to survive in the post-war years.

The 1946 model was given telescopic forks and an optional sprung hub at the rear, and in this form it produced 28bhp and weighed 182kg (400lb). This gave a lively performance with a top speed of

Did you know?
Actor James Dean bought a 1955 TR5 Trophy and this was the machine featured in a famous photo set by American photographer Phil Stern.

◄ The BSA Rocket 3 was produced after BSA became part of the Norton-Villiers-Triumph group and is effectively a version of the Trident with a different frame and sloping cylinders. It was introduced just before the Honda CB750 and its sales suffered badly as a result, but there were notable racing successes, especially in the hands of John Cooper.

Did you know?

Bob Dylan owned a Triumph Tiger 100, which he crashed in 1966. Although details of the accident and his injuries remain rather mysterious, Dylan retired almost completely from public performance for eight years.

> A motorcycle is not just a two-wheeled car; the difference between driving a car and climbing onto a motorcycle is the difference between watching TV and actually living your life.
>
> Dave Karlotski

around 100mph, depending on conditions. By the end of the 1940s, other companies were building 500cc twins, so the Speed Twin engine was given a larger bore and stroke, increasing its capacity to 650cc. Turner named this more powerful machine the Thunderbird and, initially, it was the fastest bike in the Triumph line-up.

The early Twins had a separate engine and gearbox and this was replaced by a 'Unit Construction' machine in 1957. There was also a Sports version, the Tiger 100, from 1959; the '100' representing its top speed. When the 650cc engine was fitted, the bike became the Tiger 110.

The TR5 Trophy was an off-road variant on the theme whose name derived from Triumph's team trophy won by a trio of the machines in the world famous International Six Days Trial. The 650cc TR6 Trophy was added to the range in 1956.

The 750cc T140 Triumph Bonneville and TR7 Tiger are really very similar bikes, the Bonneville being basically a twin-carburettor version of the Tiger. These machines were produced by the Meriden co-operative, following the collapse of Norton-Villiers-Triumph in 1977. The two photographed overleaf both live in Germany and are the property of Guenter Kranz who, like so many vintage bike enthusiasts, owns a collection of several machines. In Guenter's case, the collection is fifteen strong and includes no fewer than three Manx Nortons,

Guenter Kranz' Triumph Bonneville 750 with informative German number plate.

Guenther's 750cc Tiger is virtually identical to his 'Bonnie'

Did you know?

The 05/11 on the Bonneville is a money-saver, showing that this bike is only licensed for use between 1st May and 30th November. That makes sense for bikes which are stored in the winter (when time can be set aside for replacement tanks to be painted!). The vehicle is effectively SORNed when not in use, although different combinations of months are allowed under the German system.

one of which ran in the 1994 Manx Grand Prix. Guenter, who also owns a staggeringly well-equipped workshop and has a wealth of racing experience, reports that he can feel no difference in power between the two 750cc Triumph engines.

Other points of interest on this pair include the number plates; the 07– number on the Tiger indicates a vintage vehicle and attracts a lower tax rate in Germany. Unlike British plates, these also indicate that the vehicles are registered to an owner who lives in Bad Tolz, Bavaria, and that the Bonneville has passed its MOT-equivalent safety inspection. This is the upper of the two badges on the left of the plate (the brown colour even indicates that the most recent test was in 2010). The Tiger doesn't need one as it was first registered in 1980 i.e., more than thirty years ago. The other badge is the Bavarian registration seal.

Helpfully, the plate on the non-vintage machine has been kept small by the practice of deliberately allocating single letters and small numbers (T78 in this case) to the lower row when registering motorcycles.

> Cars lie to us and tell us we're safe, powerful, and in control. The air-conditioning fans murmur empty assurances and whisper, "Sleep, sleep." Motorcycles tell us a more useful truth: we are small and exposed, and probably moving too fast for our own good, but that's no reason not to enjoy every minute of the ride.
>
> Dave Karlotski

Rear suspension initially took the form of a sprung seat, and was intended purely for rider comfort rather than improving the handling of the machine.

Edward Turner, of Triumph Speed Twin and Ariel Square Four fame, designed a 'sprung hub' in 1938. This had the advantage that it could be fitted to a rigid frame without modification, but also had the disadvantages that it only allowed 2in of travel and did not permit damping. The hub's development was delayed by the war and it finally appeared on Ernie Lyons' specially prepared Triumph Tiger 100 in time for the 1946 Senior Manx Grand Prix. Lyons won the race in terrible weather conditions.

However, both 'plunger' designs and modern-type swinging arms (sometimes called pivoted forks) arrived on a few machines even before the First World War. Strangely, there are still machines

Did you know?

Early seats were sprung, much as bicycle saddles were. A disadvantage was the movement between rider and foot rests; his knees flexed over every bump. The 'Edmund' had a seat tube sliding inside the frame; the tube emerged at the bottom bracket and carried the footrests so the feet moved vertically with the saddle.

(particularly American designs) on sale with solid rear ends.

In the plunger suspension, the wheel moves vertically on two telescopic tubes containing coil springs, while the swinging arm may use two coil spring/damper units placed on either side, or a single one

placed centrally and operated by linkages or cantilevers. This latter design can give a reduction in unsprung mass and assist the suspension in its job of keeping the wheel on the ground.

The Brough Superior and the 1951 Vincent Rapide both have a 'monoshock-type' rear suspension, but actually use a *pair* of springs as seen in the pictures. (Note also that the Brough still used adjustable

◄◄ One of the more original engine layouts which have been tried by Edward Turner. The 1000cc Ariel Square Four - or 'Squariel' - is basically a pair of 500cc parallel twins geared together and with a single four-cylinder block. It was a smooth and popular machine and remained in production for almost 30 years.

◄ The rear of the 1951 BSA ZB34 showing plunger-type rear suspension.

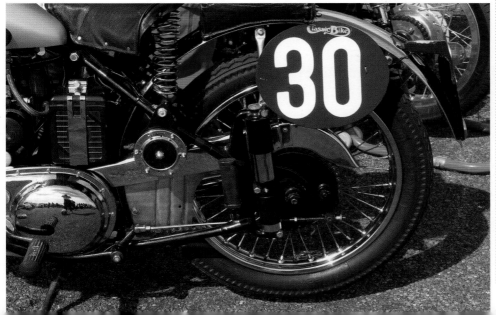

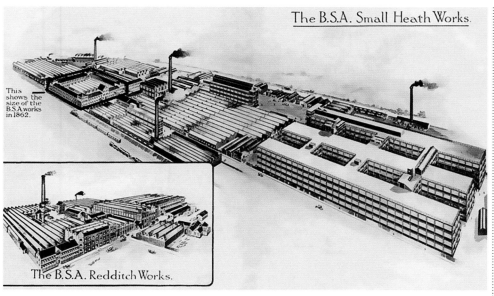

The B.S.A. Small Heath Works.

This shows the size of the B.S.A. works in 1862.

The B.S.A. Redditch Works.

<< Bill Bewley's Concours-winning 1951 Vincent Rapide.

< The impressive extent of the BSA factories in 1918 (courtesy of Grace's Guide).

I got the signal 'first by seven seconds'. This was not as big a lead
as I had expected so I went a little faster for the rest of the lap –
but not by any means extending myself or the bike.
TT star Stanley Woods in a letter to Adrian Earnshaw MHK
(courtesy of VMCC IpM/Job Grimshaw)

◀▲▶ Two very similar BSAs from 1929 and 1930. BSA launched the 'Sloper' model in 1927, so named because the engine was inclined forward to take advantage of the saddle-style tank and give a lower centre of gravity. The 5.57hp (493cc) single cylinder engine gave the H29 De Luxe version (the single seat bike here) a top speed of around 70mph.

friction damping at the rear as at the front.) These rear suspension developments can clearly be seen in BSA machines.

The single-cylinder, four-stroke, 350cc B31 of 1949, though introduced after the Second World War, is essentially a pre-war

1949 BSA 350cc B31.

The 1951 500cc 'Gold Star' version of the BSA B34 with an alloy engine.

A really beautiful example of a BSA A10.

design and has a solid rear end combined with telescopic forks at the front. It was capable of about 70mph.

By 1951, the Gold Star variant had a plunger frame, a 500cc alloy engine and was capable of well over 100mph. In fact, by the mid-1950s, such bikes were able to lap the TT course at average speeds of more than 85mph. Bear in mind that this is a 37.75-mile circuit of closed public roads, passing through towns and villages and close to the exposed summit of Snaefell Mountain. Even today it

A nice example of BSA's C15. Produced from 1958–1967 this 250cc four-stroke was, at the time, the biggest capacity machine a learner could ride in the UK.

poses a unique challenge, but the roads were much poorer in the 1950s.

The 1961 650cc Golden Flash has a much more modern-looking swinging arm rear suspension. The A10 (along with its 500cc smaller brother the A7) was a parallel twin and was produced over a seventeen-year period, with the first A7 arriving in 1946, and the last A10 model (the Super Rocket) remaining in production until 1963.

Both were originally available in rigid and plunger versions, but rigid frames were phased out across most of the BSA range by 1952. Just a few single-cylinder models were still managing without rear suspension after this time, and the Golden Flash gained its swinging arm in 1954. Along the way it also gained a headlamp nacelle, bigger brakes and an Amal Monobloc carburettor.

The A10 Super Rocket was the last of the BSA pre-unit twins; that is to say bikes with a separate engine and gearbox.

◄ BSA A10 Golden Flash sidecar outfit. This machine is fitted with an Earles-type fork. Note also the electrically-operated gear-change unit.

The Golden Flash, in particular, was also a popular sidecar machine due to its smooth and generous power delivery, and brakes which were considered strong in their day. Magazine testers stated that the brakes could easily stop the machine from high speeds. The author's own recollections of a late-model A10 were a little less reassuring, but of course then, as now, condition is all and I was an impecunious student. The rear brake pedal was on the opposite side of the machine from the actuating lever on the drum, and this necessitated a cross shaft through the frame which was prone to damage if the machine had been dropped. Very difficult to remove if bent too! Somehow though, I can't see or hear one without thinking 'I used to have one of those' and that's how we really know how good an old bike was.

One of the BSA bikes pictured has a sidecar (note the leading link front suspension – 'almost' an Earles fork) and 'Kliktronic' push-button gear-change. Luxury.

Despite its 'British bike' appeal, it has to be admitted that the original 125cc BSA Bantam was a direct derivative of the German DKW RT125, whose plans came to Birmingham in the aftermath of the Second World War. Nevertheless, in numerous forms the Bantam was in production from 1948 to 1971, a period of twenty-three years, and in its later revisions it had developed a character all of its own.

The original DKW-derived Bantam of 1948 was termed the D1. It had a 125cc engine, integral three-speed gearbox, and a 'hard tail', which is of course just the nice way of saying it had no rear suspension. At the front, however, the DKW's girder fork was replaced with a pair of telescopic legs. Ignition was provided by a Wico-Pacy or Lucas magneto and the bike was painted a drab colour termed 'mist green'.

Did you know?

Gear and brake operations were not standardised on motorcycles until the mid-1970s. Until then gear levers might be on the left or right and may have operated 'up-to-change-up' or 'down-to-change-up' – very confusing. The author remembers riding a Suzuki with a rocker change: 'Heel down for down, toe down for up'. Life is easier now.

The original 125cc BSA Bantam D1 in its original 'mist green'.

► Early advert for the BSA Bantam.

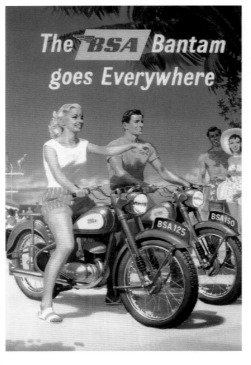

These bikes were a great success, selling in large numbers to both the general public, for whom other transport options were limited by austerity following the war, and to the GPO (General Post Office), who used them for telegram delivery.

In 1954, the D3 model appeared, offering slightly more power from its enlarged 150cc engine and plunger rear suspension. The D1 continued in production in GPO trim (now with plunger suspension added) all

I suppose that makes mine the Brough Inferior.

George Brough's father (also a motorcycle manufacturer) on hearing the name of the new Brough Superior

◄ A Bantam D7 in colours reminiscent of the GPO role these machines once fulfilled.

the way to 1968. The D3 gained a swing arm in 1956.

The 175cc engine made its appearance in the 1958 D5 model and the bike's physical appearance was updated with the D7 the following year. At this point, BSA seem to have preferred odd numbers for some reason, but in 1966 they had a change of heart and announced the D10.

Power was now up to 10bhp and the D10 'Bushman' was an off-road version with chunky tyres and extra ground clearance provided by a high-mounted engine and exhaust. These models also benefitted from coil ignition.

The four-speed gearbox arrived on the D14/4, along with a distinctive two-tone tank, and the final model (anomalously called the B175) was only a slight revision, offering such things as stronger forks (borrowed from the more powerful 250cc, four-stroke C15), a stronger kick-start and a main beam warning light.

Early models had a solo sprung seat and a parcel carrier. The modern foam-filled seat with room for a pillion passenger arrived as an option on later D1 models and was standard on the D3.

The author's first bike was a 175cc Bantam D14/4. This was chosen in 1972 from the used stock at Horners in Manchester, with the help of a more experienced friend. Always a good idea if you're only 17 and/or don't know what to look out for. This motorcycle left the factory in 1968 and it made a great introduction to biking. I took it to the Isle of Man, my first (scary) taste of the TT course.

The D14/4 really was quite a different bike from the 1948 original. The gearbox had an extra ratio (hence the '/4'), the bike had larger diameter forks at the front and

had swinging arm rear suspension. It had more power than any previous Bantam, now up to 12.6bhp, and had a claimed top speed of 65mph. There are corners on the TT course that can't be taken that fast, and maybe it was going even faster on the downhill approach to Creg-ny-Baa. The speedometer was swinging to and fro so I couldn't say, but I wouldn't have believed I could have got away with such a lean angle. I expected the skinny tyres to let go at any moment and I could almost see the old fellas sitting outside the hotel shaking their heads and hear them saying, 'Look at that young fool showing off!' – but it certainly wasn't deliberate. These are the experiences which teach you to ride more cautiously I suppose; you have to get away with them, though.

I did once try to improve the bike's performance by increasing the ignition advance a bit, and for a few minutes the result was amazing; but then it seized, so I reset it to standard. It has to be said that the engine didn't seem to come to any harm from this youthful mistreatment, so it must have been pretty tough.

The Bantam was not only good for learning to ride, but also easy for a beginner to work on. The engine was an extremely basic two-stroke single with an integral clutch and gearbox, and the whole thing was light enough to carry upstairs and strip down on a table in my bedroom. I had a very tolerant mother.

The bike was rather fussy about perfect ignition and carburation set-up, so I got plenty of experience in those areas. The carb was an Amal Concentric; a wonderful and deceptively simple design which was found, in various sizes and with appropriate jetting, on a huge range of British motorcycles of the period. Later, when I moved up to a 650cc BSA A10 Super Rocket, many things were different, but the familiar old

The great Wal Handley riding a Rex Acme 350cc machine at Creg-Ny-Baa corner during the 1926 Isle of Man TT.

The Amal Monobloc carb. This one is fitted to a BSA C15 but these were fitted to a huge number of different British bikes and are still available today.

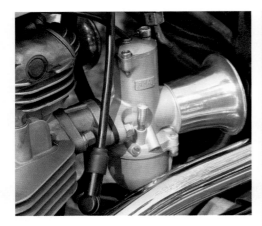

▲ The beautifully simple Concentric carburettor with float chamber, jets and throttle body all vertically aligned. Perhaps even more popular than the Monobloc.

Amal carburettors were made from the 1920s and are still available new today, as the current owners of the name (Burlen Fuel Systems Ltd) have a major commitment to supplying parts for classic British machinery.

The name itself may relate to the 'amal' gamation of several different companies in the years following the First World War. What is certain is that Amal carbs established a great reputation as essentially simple, yet solid designs which functioned well and were easily worked on by their owners.

Many of the developments made over the years were aimed at reducing manufacturing costs by further increasing this inherent simplicity.

The earliest models – known as the 'Standard' series – used float chambers which were separate from the main body, and this arrangement continued on the 'TT' and 'GP' models intended for high-performance and racing engines. The float chamber could be mounted rigidly to the main body or remotely.

In 1954 the company introduced the 'Monobloc' carb. As its name indicates, this has the float chamber incorporated in the main body, although it is set to one side of the throttle and jet assembly. The picture shows a Monobloc carburettor fitted to a BSA C15.

The 'Concentric' design made its appearance in 1967 and is a masterpiece of neatness and simplicity. The float is now vertically beneath the throttle slide and concentric with it. There was little to go wrong and, in any case, the carburettor could be removed from the bike, stripped, cleaned and reassembled in next to no time – even by an inexperienced teenage mechanic such as the author then was! This was a brilliant little carburettor which was manufactured (as all the previous models had been) in a range of sizes to fit the requirements of different engines.

The Concentric range was developed over time through Mark 1 (Zinc alloy body, cold starting by both air slide and a 'tickler' to flood the float bowl), Mark 1.5 (cold starting system with its own petrol and air supplies) and Mark 2 (aluminium body) versions and declined in popularity only as a result of the decline in British motorcycle manufacturing.

Concentric was still there. Odd really, since the bike should have been fitted with the Amal TT, but other parts were also non-standard. The tank was a rather beautiful glass fibre version originally fitted to an A65 Spitfire, and the exhausts were straight-through racing megaphones. This bike was *loud*, but as a teenager I thought it sounded great – at least after I got the mixture adjusted to stop it back-firing every time I rolled off the throttle.

In the immediate post-war years of the 1940s and '50s, money was tight, 'pool' petrol was of low quality and low octane rating (around 77), and, as a consequence, engines ran at low compression ratios and needed de-choking fairly regularly. In this climate, cars were comparatively few and motorcycles numerous. Fitted with sidecars they were family transport; solo machines got people to work.

Powerful bikes were suited to sidecar use, but something smaller was better for commuting. Two-stroke engines offered simplicity, which made them cheap to make and easy for the owner to maintain, and so most manufacturers included small two-stroke bikes in their range.

The James company was one such manufacturer; the firm produced its first motorbike in 1902 and became part of the

◄ ► Two views of the 1955 225cc James Colonel K12. Note the clean, simple lines of this bike and the unusually positioned ignition key – on top of the crankcase on the right-hand side.

AMC group in 1951. The model shown is a Colonel K12 of 1955, powered by a two-stroke Villiers engine of 225cc and finished in the typical James maroon. Note the ignition key positioned in the right-hand top surface of the crankcase, and the unusual housing for the carburettor.

The 225cc engine size enabled it to fit into a lower tax band and also made it cheaper to insure than a conventional 'just below 250cc' machine. The bike has a low seat, and it has been suggested that this served to make it more appealing to older riders. However, most older bikes were low-slung by modern standards and this is surely a reflection of the greater angles possible when cornering on modern tyres.

The BSA Bantam not only sold in good numbers right from the start, but it also inspired many owners to make modifications in order to seek a bit more performance. This inevitably led to competition; something the original designers in Germany presumably did not have in mind. Nevertheless, Bantam-based racing remains strong to the present day.

The picture on page 77 gives an extreme view of what was (and is) possible using the small BSA two-stroke as the base. This bike even has a hand-made expansion box exhaust which creates a pressure wave to 'ram' unburnt mixture back into the cylinder. This only works over a very narrow rev band,

They copied all they could follow
But they couldn't copy my mind
And I left 'em sweating and a'stealing
A year and a half behind.
Rudyard Kipling, as used in Brough
advertising

but gives a sizeable increase in power. Such pipes have to be tuned in both shape and length to give the maximum power boost and the most useful engine speed. It also makes for an engine which is difficult to use efficiently. Anyone who has seen two-stroke racing is familiar with riders slipping the clutch out of slow corners in order to keep revs up and get the engine 'on the pipe'.

This exhaust tuning has also resulted in many modern bikes having six gears. The two-stroke race bikes of the 1960s used large numbers of gears to make better use of their narrow power band and rules were introduced to limit them to six.

In fact, the competitive advantage enjoyed by Scott motorcycles in the 1920s still applies. A two-stroke engine fires once every revolution, as opposed to the four-stroke's once every two rotations, and can therefore produce more power.

As a result, the two-stroke was dominant in racing, where ultimate performance is everything, until very recently. Two-strokes even held sway in the MotoGP class, the pinnacle of motorcycle racing, until 2002 when the rules were changed to favour four-strokes. In a move which Alfred Scott would certainly have recognised, the four-strokes were given a capacity advantage. This time, however, the advantage was great enough to ensure that two-strokes could no longer compete. Two-strokes retained their existing limit of 500cc and four-strokes were allowed up to 990cc. The following year there were no two-strokes in the MotoGP field.

They did continue in the 125cc Grand Prix class right up to 2011, but again the rules were used to remove them as the class itself was replaced by Moto 3; a series for 250cc four-strokes.

This is a 32cc engine built into a bicycle wheel and though produced in the 1950s by EMI Factories in Hayes, Middlesex, it may be seen as a throwback to the very early days of powered bicycles. Like the original BSA Bantam the design originated in Germany and came to Britain after the Second World War. This one is in the A.R.E. museum, Kirk Michael, IoM.

The most likely reason for this seeming antipathy to a design which demonstrably produces more power than a four-stroke, is that it is seen as having little or no relevance outside racing. The two-stroke tends to be noisy and unreliable, and must inevitably burn its oil, and so the four-stroke has retained its position as the engine of choice in most non-racing applications. Many enthusiasts lament the passing of the 'stroker', and, with the development of solutions to its problems, it remains possible that Scott may have the last laugh.

The old Triumph company ... was in very low water and I realised ... that I had to design something that would make impact fairly immediately; I started designing what afterwards became the Speed Twin and it was an immediate success and it sold for £74.

Edward Turner, interviewed in the 1970s

As stated earlier, Velocette motorcycles are among the most highly regarded of classic machinery. Though the company was small compared to the likes of BSA, Norton and Triumph, and thus had fairly limited production, they built machines of quality and, as a result, a great many are still roadworthy.

The company's first bikes were named 'Veloce', an Italian term used as a direction in music and meaning 'to be played rapidly'. Real success came with the introduction of a range of lightweight two-strokes – the Velocettes – and this is the name which stuck, even after the return to four-strokes.

Veloce were technically innovative, introducing such modern features as the positive stop, foot-operated gearbox, the pivoted fork (swinging arm) rear suspension and a method of mounting rear shock absorbers which allows the damping and spring rates to be adjusted easily by the owner. The upper mounting point is elongated and the top end of the spring/damper unit can be moved along the slot.

Did you know?

Velocette founder John Goodman was born Johannes Gutgemann in Oberwinter, Germany. He became a British citizen in 1911 and changed his name in 1917. His sons Percy and Eugene joined the company in 1916. In later years, Percy's son, Bertie, was managing director, and Bertie's son, Simon, also worked in the factory.

➤ Ivan Rhodes' 1913 Velocette Model A pictured at the 2007 Banbury Run (courtesy of Paul d'Orleans / The Vintagent).

Towards the vertical gives stiffer springing and more damping; away from the vertical has the opposite effect. The stiffer settings are particularly useful when carrying a passenger on the pillion.

In 1925 the company pioneered the use of a strobe light in engine development; enabling the engine to be studied in motion and allowing ignition timing to be set accurately.

Velocettes were always heavily involved in competition, and always well towards the front. Their greatest milestones were back-to-back 350cc World Championships in 1949–1950 for Freddie Frith and Bob Foster, and the feat of covering 2,400 miles in twenty-four hours – thereby averaging over 100mph – which was achieved by a 500cc Venom at Montlhéry in France. This sustained speed on an OHV Single! No-one has equalled it since and the riders included the Veloce managing director, Bertie Goodman – a truly heroic performance.

An interesting Velocette customer was Graham Hill, later to be Formula One World Champion and father of Damon, also a World Champion. Graham's motor sport career began in 1948 when, aged 19, he did a small amount of motorcycle scrambling (now called motocross) on a 350cc Velocette. He didn't even learn to drive a car until almost five years later. Hill's mother had in fact ridden a Triumph 250 from the age of 17.

The 192cc Velocette LE was actually the best-selling model of all. It sold to police forces in great numbers and earned the title 'noddy bike'. Opinions vary on the reason for this; many believe that it is a reference to Enid Blyton's character who was often in trouble with Mr Plod, but there is a strong and plausible story that the term arises

Velocette MOV 250cc engine from 1937. The distinctive timing chest cover is known as the 'map of Africa' for obvious reasons and was used on all the pushrod OHV Velocette engines.

from the police themselves. Constables were instructed not to salute sergeants and officers when riding motorcycles, but simply to nod as this was obviously safer!

Sadly, the production costs of the LE were high and it was never truly profitable, though it remained in the catalogue for nearly twenty years.

Did you know?

Prior to the introduction of Compulsory Basic Training (CBT), it was legal to apply for a provisional licence and set out on the roads. If you didn't want to ride a big bike then you never needed to take a test. In the 1970s, the voluntary RAC/ACU Training Scheme provided an excellent grounding in riding. The course, which operated until 1982, took a few Saturday mornings to complete and was of enormous value. CBT for all riders only began in 1990.

◀ The 500cc Velocette Venom was produced from 1955 to 1970 and has a top speed of 100mph. More than 5,500 were sold and a considerable number survive – due at least in part to Veloce's high build quality and standard of finish.

➤ Badge awarded to those who completed the RAC/ACU training course

The early girder-type fork was remarkably long-lived. Even though manufacturers such as Scott had begun to experiment with telescopic arrangements around the time of the First World War, and BSA were using hydraulically damped telescopic forks from 1945, there were those who felt that the inherent lack of stiffness of a telescopic fork would always render them inadequate – at least for heavy and powerful motorcycles.

Chief among these were Phil Vincent and his long-time chief engineer, Phil Irving. Vincent had bought the remnants of the unprofitable HRD Motors Ltd in 1928 and renamed it Vincent HRD Co. Ltd., with Irving joining him in 1931.

Vincent motorcycles are legendary; this author first encountered one (a Black Shadow) while learning to ride on the excellent RAC/ACU Training Scheme in the early 1970s. One of the instructors rode in

on this amazing, huge – to my inexperienced eyes – black monster. For me, ever since, there has been something 'serious' about a 1,000cc V-twin, but nothing quite like a Vincent with its slow thump ('one bang per telegraph pole' was the joke) and those 'old-fashioned' girder forks which never quite looked 'right' to a youngster. My taste has improved since.

To me, still wobbling around on small machines and finding their limited power quite adequate to be going on with, the Vincent (girders or not) looked and sounded like a 'proper man's bike'. Yes I know – and I could name – many women, past and present, who have proved they can ride much better than I ever will. It's just how I felt at the time.

The V-twin engine was designed by Phil Irving, an Australian who went on to design the World Championship-winning Repco Formula One engines used by Brabham in the mid-1960s. It took the arrival of the Cosworth DFV/Lotus 49/Jim Clark combination in 1967 to push them off the top of the heap.

There is a story that Irving came up with the idea of the Vee when he accidentally placed two tracings of the existing 500cc Vincent single on top of each other with one back to front. He noticed that by carefully arranging them he could arrive at a workable layout for a 1,000cc V-twin. Personally, I prefer to think he did it deliberately, but I don't claim to know.

> [Phil Vincent] always had an extremely determined character. He was never a man with which one would wish to argue. His determination was what had led to the success of the Vincent motorcycle.
>
> Robin Vincent-Day (thevincent.com)

The V-twin was so strongly built that it enabled Vincent to take another revolutionary step in design by using it as a stressed structural component of the bike. Many of the tubes used in a conventional frame were eliminated and the overall result was extremely rigid.

I had the good fortune to meet both the son-in-law and the grandson of Phil Vincent, along with restorer and owner-of-Vincents, Bill Bewley, on the Isle of Man in 2011. Bill told me many interesting things (such as how to recognise instantly whether a Vincent still has its original engine), while Robin told me of his father-in-law's long-term, albeit unfulfilled, desire to build a ceramic engine as he so disliked seeing heat go to waste.

Series 'C' and 'D' Vincents from 1948 onwards were fitted with hydraulic dampers, and their forks were described as 'Girdraulic'. This fork can be seen clearly in

Actually, the Cosworth F1 engine came about in a similar way, combining two 1,600cc FVA engines to make a 3-litre V8.

◄◄ The stunning, Phil Irving designed, 998cc V-Twin engine looks spectacular in Bill Bewley's Rapide.

◄ 1950s Vincent Girdraulic fork. This is a 'beefed up' version of the traditional girder fork but fitted with a pair of hydraulic dampers. The two Phils, Vincent and Irving, did not consider the telescopic forks of the time to be stiff enough.

the photograph of a 1948 Black Lightning; a stripped-down racing version of the 998cc Black Shadow. Many steel parts were replaced with aluminium or removed altogether. Note the aluminium wheel rims, the racing seat, the lack of lights and the rear-set racing footrests.

The Vincent's reputation as the fastest production motorcycle was enhanced on 13 September 1948 at Bonneville Salt Flats,

when Rollie Free set a motorcycle land speed record of 150.313mph. He rode a Black Lightning, lying flat on the rear mudguard with his legs straight out behind him, the seat having been removed. To further reduce drag, he wore a pair of swimming trunks and a pair of 'sneakers'. There is clearly some kind of headgear

visible in the picture and some sources refer to this as a shower cap, but it actually looks like the 'pudding basin' helmet Free normally wore. It could only have served to reduce wind resistance in any case – if he had come off the bike he would have been skinned alive.

Although many Vincent owners place a high value on the originality of their bikes, there have been a number of 'special projects' based on them over the years. These include out-and-out racers, show specials and even a few intended for limited production. Fritz Egli is a Swiss frame designer and former racer whose 'Egli-Vincent' caused a stir in the 1960s and '70s. Today, Patrick Godet builds these machines in France, and his beautiful 'Red Shadow' is pictured at the Vintage Motorcycle Club's Manx Grand Prix Festival in 2011.

◁ The Egli-Vincent Red Shadow is surely one of the most magnificent-looking motorcycles ever made.

If it would have made it go faster I would have stood up on it.
Rollie Free

We have considered suspension development in some detail already, but the best suspension in the world only works as well as the frame it is attached to. Early bicycle-type frames fulfilled the basic requirements of holding all the major parts in suitable positions, but as engines became more powerful, so the forces on the frame also increased and this caused both breakages and problems of excessive flexibility.

Did you know?

Comedian George Formby, who starred in the TT-based film *No Limit*, owned several motorbikes, including a Norton International which was presented to him at the factory in 1947.

▶ Two views of Simon Smith's spectacular-sounding 1947 350cc Manx Norton. This is a relatively rare pre-featherbed 'Garden Gate' model.

A simple improvement was to use thicker tube and larger welds, but this made frames heavier and did not in itself solve the problem of breakage. Many people worked on solutions to these issues, but Belfast's Rex McCandless stands head and shoulders above the rest.

The Norton company was one of the oldest motorcycle manufacturers in the world and had a strong racing pedigree, having entered machines in every Isle of Man TT since the event became a 'motorcycle-only race' in 1907.

In the 1930s, Norton motorcycles won many TTs, and Norton riders such as Jimmie Guthrie and Stanley Woods were household names, just as Jorge Lorenzo and Valentino Rossi are today.

The 'Manx' Nortons were tuned versions of the Norton International model (also known as the Model 30 or the 'Cammy') and were powered by an overhead cam, single-cylinder engine of either the 'Junior' 348cc or the 'Senior' 499cc. A double overhead cam version appeared in 1937 and this engine, developed for racing by Norton's engineer, Joe Craig, was to remain fundamentally competitive for many years.

> I never had any formal training. I came to believe that it stops people from thinking for themselves.
> Rex McCandless (The Vintagent. blogspot.co.uk)

However, by the late 1940s, Norton had a problem. Their engine was excellent but their plunger frames were not; they handled badly and broke frequently. Joe Craig's efforts to cure these problems by adding material had only made them heavier.

Meanwhile, over in Ireland, Rex McCandless, having left school at 13 years old, and having no engineering qualifications, had designed a racing frame and built a bike around it. This frame used a swinging arm

at the rear and a pair of hydraulic dampers from a car. It handled so well that he produced a conversion kit for rigid framed bikes and began to establish a reputation.

McCandless made contact with Norton and claimed that he had a frame which was better than theirs. A test was arranged on the Isle of Man, with Geoff Duke riding

◀◀ This Triton (a Triumph Speed Twin engine in a Norton featherbed frame) uses many new parts, probably including the frame, but it is unquestionably a genuine Triton for all that.

◀ Another beautiful Triton standing alongside an unusual Vincent Special.

the plunger machine and Artie Bell on the McCandless. The rest, as they say, is history. Norton's engine was given a new lease of life and they enjoyed 1-2-3 finishes in both the Junior and Senior TTs of 1950.

The name 'featherbed' was given to the McCandless frame by Harold Daniell, one of the leading riders of the day, after riding one. It is certainly more flattering than the 'garden gate' nickname of the original Norton plunger!

The featherbed frame consists of two separate components, each very roughly rectangular, and each formed from a single length of Reynolds tubing. The ends of each tube cross over each other at the front, and the head bearing tube is then welded to the four protruding ends. The rear wheel is supported by a swinging arm and a pair of spring/shock absorber units; the result is a chassis which provides great strength and rigidity relative to its weight.

A patent was applied for in 1949 and granted in 1952.

The 'Manx' Norton is now regarded as legendary, and the featherbed frame became the basis for later versions (1951 Model 88 onwards) of the 'Dominator' road bike.

In fact, the original frames were effectively of third-party manufacture, since Norton did not have the welding capability to make the racing featherbed themselves. The lightweight Reynolds tubing required sif-bronze welding and Rex McCandless, never a Norton employee, brought his own jig (which still exists) over from Belfast and built the frames required by the works racing team himself.

Later, mild steel frames for road use were welded more conventionally using steel filler rod. Even so, welding motorcycle frames remains a job for the experienced.

In fact, there were two versions of the featherbed for road use: in its original

◁ Another take on 'one-engine-in-the-frame-of-another'. The Tri-Greaves is a Speed Twin motor in a Greaves scrambler with a leading link fork.

CAFÉ RACERS

The 1950s and '60s saw the development of a phenomenon known as the café racer. This was the era of Rock 'n' Roll, and it was also a time, soon after the war, in which the teenager was becoming a recognised group in society.

Teenagers had money to spend, but cars were too expensive. Motorbikes offered an unbeatable combination of excitement and rebellion at a price which many could afford. The practical requirement to wear leather only added to the desired image – especially if the leather was decorated with badges and slogans. The term 'café racer' stems from the practice (illegal and dangerous of course, and therefore highly attractive) of racing from 'cafe to cafe' or from 'cafe to roundabout and back'. If the rider could achieve the 'ton' (100mph) at some point along the route he was seen as belonging to the elite.

It needs to be realised that simply reaching 100mph was far more difficult on the bikes of the period (and on the roads of the period) than on a modern superbike with its massive power, excellent handling and superb brakes. Only the faster machines then could reach the magic ton and stopping was not too easy either. Accidents and fatalities were fairly frequent and the police took an understandably dim view of the whole thing.

The bikes used were many and varied. Essentially, any proper motorbike was allowed, with 'proper' effectively meaning 'not a scooter', since these were the preserve of the despised mods; a fashion-conscious teen group who would not be seen in scuffed leather.

Riders were keen to customise their bikes, both to make them distinctive and to make them faster. Racer-style features, such as low handlebars (known as clip-ons, since they are clamped separately to the fork tubes rather than running across the top of the yoke), tuned engines and loud exhausts; these add-ons and many others were common and produced a look which can clearly be seen as the precursor of the road-going superbike.

A modern re-enactment of the café racer craze is active in many places today, especially the USA, where restored or replica British bikes are in demand. Often these modern-day café bikes are fitted with exotic engines, such as Guzzi V-twins, which few British riders of the 1960s could possibly have afforded. However, the style of the bikes is retained and no doubt the original café bikers would have been more than happy with them. Certainly the ton no longer poses a problem.

form the frame was quite wide at the top and many riders found it uncomfortable sitting with their knees that far apart; in the 'slimline' version, the top tubes are closer together. This also makes the frame slightly lighter, and also slightly less stiff.

So revolutionary was the featherbed that it quickly became the basis for a raft of hybrid machines during the era of the 'café racer', where a variety of different engines could be fitted. Hence, with a Triumph engine we have the 'Triton'. Other combinations include machines such as the 'NorBSA' and 'NorbStar' bikes with BSA engines. Rarer featherbed-based specials even include the 'NorVin' with a mighty Vincent Black Shadow powerplant. As the Vincent engine was capable of acting as a stressed member of the frame, the lower tubes of the Norton frame were sometimes removed.

Featherbed frames are still available new, as several specialist manufacturers produce them from the original specification. These bikes look superb and it may be expected that, with modern additions, such as stronger brakes, they are even better than the originals.

◀ The name on the tank says it all. You won't see a nicer TriBSA than this.

It seemed obvious to me that the rigidity of the frame was of paramount importance. .... Of equal importance was that the wheels would stay in contact with the road. That may seem obvious, but fast motorcycles then bounced all over the place. I decided that soft springing, properly and consistently damped, was required.

Rex McCandless (The Vintagent.blogspot.co.uk)

My selection of classic motorcycles cannot be complete without consideration of Royal Enfield – arguably the oldest surviving motorcycle manufacturer anywhere. In 1851, George Townsend set up a needle making business in Hunt End, near Redditch in Worcestershire. His son, George Junior, followed the path we have seen before; he began to make parts for bicycles and even invented and patented a new form of saddle.

By 1890, however, the firm was in financial trouble. Townsend left, but the company's fortunes were revived by a contract to supply rifle parts to the Royal Small Arms Factory in Enfield, Middlesex, and the name was changed to The Royal Enfield Manufacturing Co. Ltd soon afterwards.

The first powered vehicle from the factory was a car with a De Dion engine, which rolled out in 1898, and a motorcycle followed in 1901. This had a 150cc engine fitted above the front wheel, and, by the start of the First World War, Enfield were building some very smart-looking bikes with V-twin JAP engines.

With the onset of war, Enfield were contracted to supply motorcycles to the armed forces and their sidecar outfits

Did you know?

J.D. Wetherspoon re-opened the old cinema in Redditch as a pub in 2010. It is called 'The Royal Enfield' and, at the time of writing, owners of late-model Royal Enfield (post-1999) machines can enjoy a discount on food by producing their branded key.

carried machine guns into battle. There was also a stretcher-bearing version and Enfield started producing its own engines – although they were still fitting JAPs in some models several years later.

By the mid-1920s, there were Enfield machines with two- and four-stroke engines, and sidecar outfits, and this range, with solid build quality and modern appearance, continued to sell through the hardships of the 1930s.

The Second World War again saw Royal Enfield machines ordered in great numbers and this time they included the 'Flying Flea', a 125cc machine which looked rather like a miniature BSA Bantam. This isn't surprising since, like the Bantam, it was developed from a German DKW design!

The Flea was designed to be dropped from an aircraft along with airborne troops, thus allowing them to move quickly on the ground. For this purpose, it was supplied with its own parachute and a 'birdcage' structure to protect it on landing.

However, the most famous model name associated with Royal Enfield is the 'Bullet'. The first Bullet was a single-cylinder machine and was introduced in 1931. This model featured exposed valves and was made in both 350cc and 500cc variations.

The 250cc Bullet, made in 1933, was quite different, having a girder fork, saddle tank and a solid rear end. The bike achieved its present-day form in 1949 with a 350cc single-cylinder engine, telescopic forks and swinging arm rear suspension. The 350cc machine's strong engine made it a successful trials bike; success which increased further with the appearance of a 500cc alternative in 1953.

In 1954, the Indian government placed an order for 800 Bullets. This stretched the factory to its limit and, when similar orders arrived in 1955 and 1956, the decision

was made to set up a factory in India. The workers were trained in Redditch to produce the 1955 Bullet and, in effect, they continued to do so for many years. Enfield India Ltd, who now own the rights to the Royal Enfield name, have responded to developments in materials and manufacturing over the years, and have sometimes been forced to change the bikes in the face of legislation; nevertheless, they have retained the look and feel of the Bullet their customers love. Only in very recent times has a Unit Construction engine and gearbox been introduced with five gears, and the gear lever moved to the left side of the machine. The Bullet Standard 350 ceased production for the European market in 2007 due to ever more stringent emission laws, but the new lean-burn, all-aluminium, Unit Construction engines have ensured that the Royal Enfield Bullet, which has been exported in vast numbers to at least twenty countries, should remain on the scene for a long time yet. You can even still get it with a sidecar. Sadly, it isn't made in Redditch any longer – how times change.

◀ Both these bikes may look like old timers, but the Royal Enfield Bullet 300 actually left the factory in India not so very long ago – 2001 in fact.

In war there is an obvious need for transport; not only for guns and ammunition or even large groups of soldiers, but also for individuals. In both world wars, reliable communication, for example, could still depend on men or women physically carrying messages from place to place, since electronic methods could easily be disrupted.

The motorcycle was small, light and relatively easy to maintain, and thus it was widely used. In the First World War, the Triumph Model H was used extensively by army despatch riders, and over 30,000 were produced specifically for this purpose. It required virtually no modification to withstand the rigours of military life, although it was found that large bumps could cause damage to the front suspension spring. Riders quickly began to add a leather strap as a form of 'bump stop', and that was about all that was needed.

The Motor Machine Gun Service was formed in 1914 during the early part of the war, when it was realised that batteries of highly mobile machine guns could be of real value. Each battery consisted of eighteen Clyno or Royal Enfield motorcycle/sidecar combinations, carrying six Vickers Maxim machine guns and supported by eight solo Triumph motorcycles and a small number of cars or trucks.

However, the sidecar did not provide a stable enough platform for a machine gun and, in order for it to be fired, it was removed from the outfit and fitted to a tripod. A gun-carrying motorcycle actually went into battle with two other machines without guns to carry fuel, ammunition and spare parts – and to provide backup if the lead machine broke down.

The Clyno company had been in dire financial straits at the start of the war,

Not all old machines are lovingly restored to showroom condition! This Norton seems to have a story to tell though. Take a look at the horn ... (overleaf)

121

but the War Office contract enabled the firm to survive for a time. However, they also entered into an agreement with the Russian government to supply mobile machine-gun units, as well as ammunition carriers and solos. Unfortunately for Clyno, these were never paid for and contributed in part to Clyno's demise soon after the war. Matchless, who were not given a contract with British forces, actually built 100 similar motorcycle/machine-gun combinations for the Russian Army, but following the revolution in 1917 these were not delivered – and eventually saw service with British troops.

In the Second World War, motorcycles again played their part. Many of the major manufacturers were there, with Triumph, Norton, Matchless, BSA, Velocette, James and Rudge all represented. BSA, as the largest manufacturer, supplied a total of 126,000 M20 machines to the British armed forces over the war years.

As might be expected, the other British maker with its roots in armaments – British Enfield – also produced motorbikes for military applications, and these included the famous 125cc 'Flying Flea', which could be dropped from an aircraft in order to increase the mobility of airborne troops.

Did you know?
Wal Handley, winner of four TTs and a Brooklands Gold Star, was killed in a flying accident in the Second World War while serving with the Air Transport Auxiliary.

Despite having its factory destroyed during the Coventry Blitz, Triumph moved to premises in Meriden and, in addition to producing many thousands of bikes, also made aircraft parts; just as Clyno had during the previous conflict.

What does the future hold for the motorcycle? Much of what is happening at present is dictated by the move to greener transport, and unless a clean, quiet two-stroke engine can be developed – and this could possibly happen – the choice would seem to be between four-stroke petrol engines and the newly emerging electric machines.

This author is far from convinced by the green credentials of electric power. Not only does it have to be generated somewhere, leading to 'hidden' emissions, but far worse are the problems of manufacturing and disposing of the batteries.

In any case, the eerie silence of an electric bike as it passes by robs it of much of the spectacle; and to an enthusiast the spectacle matters.

No matter what the motorcycle of the future looks like, and no matter how it is powered, there remains another big question: who will make it?

The British bikes celebrated in this book ruled the roost until the Japanese invasion of the 1960s. Will the Japanese domination survive the coming decades? Chinese motorcycles are arriving on our shores and they will surely get better. Indeed, there are interesting times ahead.

American rider Mark Miller on his way to victory in the 2010 TT Zero race on the electrically powered MotoCzysz E1pc.

Ansell, David, *The Illustrated History of Military Motorcycles (Osprey, 1996)*
Currie, **Bob**, *Great British Motorcycles of the Fifties* (Chancellor Press, 1980)
Jones, **Barry**, *Granville Bradshaw: A Flawed Genius?* (Panther Publishing, 2008)
Walker, **Mick**, *BSA Pre-Unit Twins: The Complete Story* (The Crowood Press, 2005)

Grace's Online Guide to British Industrial History – www.*gracesguide.co.uk*
The Vintagent/Paul D'Orleans – www.*thevintagent.blogspot.co.uk*

Other titles available in this series

THE HMS VICTORY STORY

■ ISBN 978 07524 5605 8

THE QE2 STORY

■ ISBN 978 07524 5094 0

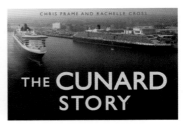

THE CUNARD STORY

■ ISBN 978 07524 5914 1

THE QM2 STORY

■ ISBN 978 07524 5092 6

THE GREAT LINERS STORY

■ ISBN 978 07524 6452 7

THE MARY ROSE STORY

■ ISBN 978 07524 6404 6

A B C D
England E F G
H I J K L
London M N O P Q R
Willows P Q R
at Christmas

Christmas
oh Christmas
Christmas
Eve

Defence of The
Realm